FIRST MOMENTS

First Moments

Poems by Robert MacIsaac

EVERY BOOK PRESS

MMXXIV

ISBN 979-8-9906539-0-0

Cover drawing by Solee MacIsaac.
Book Design by William Bentley.

Poems

"Let every day be the last,
and every moment the first."

Ilan Beth

for Sheila Wallace

Familiar visions rush past my windshield
As homeward now the pace of day escorts me;
Again the cast-iron gate, houses white and gray,
Clumps of bush border, tilting pines, a stolid oak,
Spread and rise and spread of land, ditches and fence
    posts,
Poles and letterboxes, cars abandoned or forgotten,
Bins and boulders, lawns and grazing beasts,
All these barely registered flicks of sight
Racing past at well-assured velocity;
The skimming tips of forest outline flashing apace,
The shifting leer and smile and frown of cloudy faces
Jeering or ignoring from afar my tunneled haste,
Which now devours before it digit after digit
Of the broken white stripe and the asphalt chute I
    hurtle through,
And a tiny little bird alights on the roadside edge,
And espies a something somewhere on a spot
Toward which unimpeded my vehicle is barreling hard,
And he but lightly hops out to the center way and stops,
And I am only seconds from crushing his fragile little
    frame,
And he pokes at a speck of something visible to him
    alone,
But then I see him not, the car frame loses him under,

Until the next instant he flutters up before me,
And, his footling morsel triumphantly secure,
Lifts aloft in seconds and vanishes to his airy world and
　　home.
And I remain careening through this life; and amid
The flicks of sight and sound, the blur of taste and smell,
An outline firm or faint appears of unknown
　　apprehensions:
Moments of naked heart; of soft untouchings of this
　　fleshy frame;
Elongated, lingering stillnesses immersed in fragrant
　　union;
Illumined trembling moments replete from every
　　pore;…
These, and more, the footling morsels I will gather,
　　visible to me alone,
The wings aloft which I will sail, while he who hurtles
Minds his hurried way and startles not this quiet
　　gathering.

Gazing about the library on a quiet morning,
Ticks of the clock curiously frame the silence,
Mahogany shelves and panels hold the mild light,
And hold these rows and rows of muted volumes;
Spines, many faded, most of blue or gray hue,
An occasional pink or mustard or lime winking its
    presence,
Titles just unreadable from where I sit,
Silent they stand, pressed and tucked flush with the
    edge,
Each to the other arranged in orders more of mind
    than eye.
This I regard, absorbing the reassuring surround of
    bindings,
Lingering over a familiar volume, recalling its
    atmosphere and ideas,
Recalling the presence (or absence) of its author,
Perhaps recalling the little adventure that brought it to
    this room;
Lingering then over the strangers on these shelves,
The ones as yet untouched, or opened only to breathe
    their odor and texture,
Assessing the moment when those thoughts,
    experiences,
Years, centuries ago perhaps, will enter into my life –

In some cases tomorrow, in some cases never,
The enigma of when and how we resonate with
    another's mind –
And this impression now stopping me with wonder:
What is a book, after all? A missive, personal and
    private;
A landscape tended to ripeness; a pageant cut in high
    relief of feeling;
Someone's need to not let slip an incident or memory,
However inconsequential it may have seemed to
    others;
Calls of urgent beauty, of more urgent arousal
To who and why we are, and of what we partake;
Serene reflections, whose nativity was as much a
    surprise
To the author as to his readers ages hence.
But once those words were written, with either pen or
    key tap,
Or pacing aloud while another all inscribed,
Once an image, discourse, story shaped itself
Around the special nuance only that voice could share,
Sure there followed a silence, untouchable and still,
As thought, now clothed, brought forward into light,
The delicious instant captured, like a sphere, a halo,
Alive only between those lines, afire only on that page,
But eluded if o'erpondered, or possessed of other
    explications;
And here the lesson, the secret lesson perhaps, of any
    written word,

That not their lyrics, their narration, their punchlines
    and contentions,
Their elongated logic or unadorned Muse,
Not these the message, not these the author's purpose,
    or final statement;
Instead, all sentences, all phrases, longing to build, to
    well up toward those silent gleams,
Understood in silence, and conveyed in silence, and
    read in silence.
And so the volumes keep their rest, mellowed by the
    early sun,
Silent not because open pages are not absorbing
    someone's fancy,
Not because passages are not read aloud to a friend or
    audience,
Not because no inspired pen is flying with commentary
    on phrases or insights,
But, as the soft tick of the clock inconspicuously
    measures and dies each second,
Leaving behind a momentary brushstroke of time, and
    no time,
So these ordered shelves encase their quiet gemstones
    of nothingness,
The secret of their silence between each page, each
    word,
The secret of their passing to other hearts and minds,
    the lesson of release:
To read, and let go, to linger not over what is said or
    shown,

To inhale rather, with inconspicuous certainty,
As the pages are closed, as the book is tucked away into
　　its anonymous corner,
The lively aura of the unspeakable, the silences no word
　　could ever say.

How do you know no one wrote before what you are
   reading now?

How do you know someone else did not have the exact
   same thought, and expressed it in the exact same
   way?

How do you know your sorrow was not also that of
   someone else, or of many others, and that they
   exorcised their pain in the same way you have; or
   they have not exorcised it, in the same way you have
   not?

How do you know no one carefully eyed a tree, or vase,
   or profile, and rendered it in pen or chalk or oil just
   as you did?

How do you know your poem is not another's poem; or
   was not another's poem decades or ages gone; or will
   be another's poem decades or ages to come?

How do you know no one else tasted the sea air as you
   have;

or lifted their faces to the soft misty rain like you;

or, like you, breathed mild hints of fragrance, so
   particular and so elusive, as you wandered through a
   garden;

or wrapped their arm about their loved one, and
   pressed them close, and mingled breath and kisses,
   just like you;

or sat alone on a park bench and watched anonymous
  others, and wished for companionship;
or laughed and argued with the crowd, blithely
  joked and reminisced and parted, and wished for
  companionship;
or, in an inconspicuous, unheralded moment relived
  an episode from your past, and, startled by the
  obvious, now see and understand what you had not
  seen nor understood before, and you are crushed or
  enlightened by this;
or walked out on the road or pavement in confusion
  or despair and knew no way from your wounded
  turmoil;
or sat with a friend at evening and wanted nothing
  more than this, and know you need so much this
  wanting nothing more than this;
just like you?

You could say, it never happened with the same people
  or in the same places;
You could say that only for me did it happen in this
  order, in this sequence of events;
You could say you know it did not happen, or that you
  do not care, or even that you do not know;
Whatever else you could say by way of reply, you
  always say one thing by way of reply, because you
  always are this reply:
That you, who read this now, and occupy this locus of
  space and time,
To you has come all that has come, in its own relentless

yet auspicious manner, silent, unproclaimed, for you
alone and to you alone, these moods, these deeds;
And whether you feel you are these things, or feel you
are not these things, here they have settled, here they
have come and gone, only here, in this special place
of space, of time, this place, that is only you.

Dream Rascal

No matter how many times I call to you –
You, who engenders all dreams, absent starings, futile
　　fervors,
Cravings for joys long past and fulfillments that soon
　　must, but never will, be –
No matter how often I beg you to turn and smile at me,
Or ask you to draw near and comfort my distress,
Or answer all doubt with insouciant disregard,
Or steal for me a minute, a minute more, any and all
　　minutes deemed inconsequent;
Or wish for you to fill my idle hour with phantoms
　　sweet,
Phantoms to cloy about a whimsy, to cast a sheen of
　　solace over a thought unsettled,
Phantoms to make real what should, what must, what
　　can oblige
Momentous aspirations – and live them, breathe them,
　　taste them, and have them not.
All this you give, all this and more,
An abundance of emptiness unfettered,
Perfumed sheaves to deck and adorn the altar of
　　"Somewhere Else,"

A teasing promise to trust that what is not, is, almost,
    just...almost.
And however much my inattentive yearnings
Displace my only simple instant life;
However much I wish away what is, for what you tell
    me
In an effervescent future second shall be,
You linger, and you linger, and you never ever stay.
I do not want you. No one wants you.
You are – in a final ironic turn – what no one has ever,
    ever wanted.
Goodbye, forever, thou who never wast.

 ## *Impatient Reader of Poetry*

Impatient reader of poetry,
Who, like each of us, begins to read,
And then skims down a few lines,
And then skips ahead to the final words,
And then, perhaps, sometimes with reluctance,
Or curiosity, or ennui, or impatience,
Comes back to line one, and reads,
Struggling at each line to keep it moderate,
A leisurely, non-hasty, non-feverish, non-impatient
    pace,
To arrive at this singular, uneventful punctuation.
Impatient reader, why do you skip around,
Why do any of us skip around,
Why allow a glimpse to stand for a moment,
Why expect a moment to be more than it is,
Or why assume that one moment, one line,
Is not more than it is?
What will happen next that cannot happen now?
What did happen a few lines ago that will never come
    again?
What is happening, right now, as you read this?
Whatever it is, it is not on this page,
Whatever it is, it is not in your hands,

Whatever it is, you must look for it in the right
    direction.
Impatient reader, we so often wait for it to be over,
When this is over, we can move on to what next begins,
Or move on to what we had set briefly aside,
Or move on, too often, to what we think we should
    move on to;
Or, we may pause to recall, or decide, or hesitate over,
What to do next, what we must – if we must – do next.
But, what is over? And why did we want it to be over?
Impatient reader, let us forget these names and labels.
Let us rather say, impatient viewer, impatient laborer,
Impatient pupil, impatient lover, impatient person,
Impatient someone, seeking for what is not right here,
Impatient for what is unfinished,
Impatient against what obstructs us,
Impatient for what is missing, or lacking, or
    misunderstood, or lost;
Impatient...for what is not.
Impatient reader, stop waiting for it to be over.

 ## *Fire*

A Living Myth

A long time ago in the land of Ur
There lived a man who carried fire. He bore
It not upon a brand, nor with a branch
Of candles, nor from a swaying chain,
Nor in a polished lamp of fragrant oil;
He bore it in his hands, dancing crimson
And translucent, wayward shimmering
Predictless in its sacred unrepose;
Or, leaping torch-like about his shoulders,
A florid halo throbbed heated pulses,
Shuddering tongues sudden with tameless ire.
As one espies a distant signal flare,
Or lighthouse seen from the rude, black sea,
So did the town folk watch him on the hills
As he and his dancing companion neared
The village along the narrow road,
His only purpose the simple pleasures
Of commerce and friendly sojourn;
So oft the writhing tongues about him
Made supernatural a common deed:
To talk to him was to engage a star,
And while he often had no need of speech,

Few about him easily endured
His blaze of warm, ecstatic silence,
Confounding quiet with urgent unrest.
His industry too was magic simple:
The glass and pottery adorning
His shelves and cupboards and window ledges,
The black fields of his land wet with sweet
October rain, the morning loaves of bread
That cooled on his broad wooden table,
The snapping coals in his hearth in winter,
The boiling broth in his hammered kettle;
All were the offspring of his lively burden.
He walked, and was as Nature – rosy blush
At dawn, noontide sun and celestial air,
Wily will-o-the wisp cavorting at dusk,
Spangled eyes at even – he was this,
And all who approached him glowed or aspired
As they bore witness to what could not be.
Yes – no one can hold it thus, you say.
No one can catch the dancing spark and make
It yield, no open palm will blithely couch
The nimble tongue and not be incurled wax
To its incitement. No grip so strong and
Yet so light, as air to iron, could so enfold
This trembling ether, this the blood of angels.
No man can carry fire.
                              So felt he so himself,
And oft denied what impossibly existed.
He claimed it did not follow his emergence
From the gum and water, nor that it was

A blight of youth, nor prank of clumsy
 Circumstance: "There is a valley called
"Forever – for I have no other name
"To tell – where sand and peak and plashing spring
"Alike inhale the sun. And I was there
"With staff and flask and silence for a compass.
"What raises me to tell you this, what raises
"You to hear; what other tongue with
"Other measure knew these words before;
"What people foreign to themselves pretend
"My speech is paper; what you derive and
"Call 'yourself'; what flowers seed the wind
"Indifferent …Oh love! You see I cannot
"Speak. Silence is all words. I returned again
"To my cottage and parted my hair and
"Dried my cambric on the rocks. You see what
"I am, and you turn and smile as before."
 He walked along the hills at morningtide,
 Leading his timid sheep across the green;
 While he called to his dogs and gathered stones
 In piles, the wavering flame perched about him
 As he modestly kept to his labor,
 Each movement leaving its meteoric trace.
 And to the town he came with sacks of grain,
 Or a wagonload of milk in pails, and
 People spoke to him and clutched his hand, and
 The warmth about his breast and throat was tears
 To some and trust to many. Sometimes too
 The children nestled there, but shielded their eyes
 In the noon of his embrace. The roads and

Boulevards were silent as he passed, while
The translucent orange squirmed and crackled
Under the crook of his arm, or roiled
Like a globe of light between his cautious hands.
He never dared to pass it on, nor did
Any unsteady hand outstretch itself,
Save to bask in this supernal summer.
Shops were silent as he bartered his goods,
Taverns were silent as he ate and drank;
And though he would turn and regard with love
The many looks and sometime fearful gazes,
These silent friends did not distract him from
His intercourse with the simple deed
Of the moment, nor would the flames withdraw
Their aura, nor leave his brow for other tapers.
Many were the foiled comprehensions,
Many the confusions and unvoiced pleading
Of whence this aureate brooding, and a will
That could enshrine a daemon tremulous,
This, destroyer and conceiver both.
                                        And why
Was all else unchanging – the county fair,
The Sunday sermon, shoes and purses,
 Spending and eating? Why was it all the same,
 While this one was porting the impossible?
"If I walk into the hills and observe
"The sun with shaded eyes, it stays its place
"As I do mine. I am ready for the fire,
"Yet it stays its place and I stay mine" –
This the unspoken concern of many.

When they implored him to explain, often
In the tavern while he supped, the hearth
Of his replies would make a few recline
With drooping lash and dreamy smiles, sated
With seeming reassurance; others recoiled
In singed confusion, flecks of discontent
Their only sparks of recompense; still
Others masked with coy assent a smoldering doubt
And silently probed for legerdemain,
This miracle to them no less a trick
Than desert wavers chiding an oasis.
Mostly, he was still. A slender jet quivered
In place above his shoulders and crown,
Its incandescent tips gently pulsing
Like white lips pursed for their invisible love.
He would reach for his cup and the flame
Gently shuddered; he spoke and it slowly receded,
Only to rise anew and kiss the darkness.
Once or twice a trembling hand would proffer
Itself across the table toward him,
And the light would make it visible to all;
The hand would thus remain a time and cast
A quiet shadow, and then withdraw.
"The staves, and logs, and wicks of worship
"All bear this light that clings to you. We carry
"It for our food and comfort, we strike it
"From stubborn rock, wrest it from exertion
"And dry grass, chart its majesty above.
"Where it abides is life. We cannot bring
"You where we wish to go, but often where

"We wish to go is where you sit. To deny
"The flame's presence, deny your candled gaze,
"Were to abjure a kiss of sunlight hope
"For our selfish lidded ruminations;
"We do not seek another morning than
"The one you bring. Yet were that morning
"To arise in splendor on my own brow,
"I could not ask for further sustenance
"Than the hungry blaze itself has for air.
"We struggle, and are still. You – are still.
"Teach us." This the question again and again,
This the wish, the extended hand, the service
To his plate and cup.
                        If passion ever
Had repose while still not sated, if wildness
Ever pondered its intentions even
In the wayward act, if rage and reason
Were as one, and both benevolence yet
Still caprice, it was demonstrate in this,
The flame of which they spoke. And what each person
Knew of it is what would make them burn.
He never asked them why they gathered round him:
He beheld his yellow glow reflected
In their vibrant faces. He would answer:
"When is it boredom to apprise the day?
"When is negligence the fruit of effort?
"As many Pentecosts with fiery tongue
"Describe to you your purpose, as you see
"Quavering now on every torch about
"These walls. Peruse your own fire, and watch what

19

"Rises aloft from out the kindled need
"Of your assent. I glow with reaching, and
"A wish to not stand timid in the wind,
"Nor beg a lost meaning from the cinders
"Of my regret. The diamond only cuts
"Our refulgence into fretted colors,
"The mirror only throws a shadowed guile
"That fast pretends our suppleness. No longer
"Seek a reflected life. Long ago I knelt
"Forever and only rose again when
"I was lighter than my fever. Your heat
"Is in your trials and your treasures;
"I, not water anymore."
                              So he ended.
When words are stone, man and woman bleed, though
They know it not; when words are flesh, they know
Not their embrace; and when the speech is fire,
They know not whence a sudden inner glint
Abruptly clears our accidental life
With flame – a touchless gentle luster,
Precious for its holy flickerless jet,
Held by never holding, measureless
No matter its seeming brevity:
A second becomes a year; a minute, a life.
And when such moments darkly receded,
The people's love did not. An answer radiant
From his blazing voice was not finality:
No argument laundered their confusion,
Nor did reverence become a reason. To read
O'er his words in plaintive or unearnest hours

Was to pretend. And many did, and bore
An arid sentiment and brittle mouth,
And titled it their incandescence. Yet
When he came again, the pyre of his stature
Heaved with new arousings, there was only
One joy and one light, and the sun was not
The moon.
        Eternity is motionless.
The day is but the mercy of forever.
At one time there was meaning in a road,
And the tomorrow of its horizon;
And hours measured progress, escape to joy,
Flight from clouds of reason; to live was but
To walk, and nothing in us rested save
The wish to walk again. And then there came
A fire. Then we saw the holy fingers
Snatch their wild light at silence, hurl aloft
Their scarlet rain, and pepper hooded eyes
With brightness painful in its fascination.
It always hurts to look on light. It always
Hurts to know what we must know. How fervent
Is the fire; rush and fever is not progress,
Nor voyage after passion. No – passion
Itself. The flame of day plays havoc
With the void, but we journey not forward
Nor behind. We have never left where we
Implore. How could the fire walk from its oil?
He mentioned this so gently once, "The Present
"Is your wish. Burn still, and mind not the winds
"That make you waver." Lessons are not easily

Held; sooner walk a sunbeam. He passed through
The portal of the town one afternoon
And looked back once, some later said in sorrow.
He asked that no one follow. The loved ones
Made him pause an instant to warm anew
Their purpose. This with love he granted,
And only asked that they remember all.
Sudden came a lambent, happy gesture –
Light impossible farewell – and he was gone.
To this day the massive oaken gates
Are black with that departure.

                                 East of Ur

Upon a distant hill where he once walked
There tremulous stands a column of flame,
Not flinted, fed, nor fanned by mortal deed;
Translucent licks of borealis sheen,
Radiance crimson, orange, amber, gold,
Mount in everclimbing furnace divine,
Heat perpetual, dawn on dawn unfolding,
Wisdom restraining riot celestial,
Ever tireless in its rising silence.
And to this column people came, and come,
And gaze or gesture as their awe permits;
And when for each a lingering sight imparts
An ether tinct of fire to forehead clean,
Anon the pilgrim wends his purpose homeward,
New harbored within the pleasured instant,
Reverence marking every footfall home.
This column knows each soul who passes by,
And knows as well the peoples, grim or frail,

From distant lands who never know his flame,
But only fancy it from mouths of others.
Every year the flame grows higher, brighter,
As the people of Ur more silent swell,
As touch of another's hand or lip,
And look in eye, and warmth in other's breast
Is now become the pyre that lights them all.

Stand outside me.
Move not when I move.
Ponder not what I think.
Fulfill not what I dream.
Speak not what I say.

Stand beside me.
Stop me when I move.
Halt what I think.
Dissolve what I dream.
Unvoice what I would say.

Stand alone.
Follow what shall not move.
Engage what may not think.
Incite what cannot yearn.
Repeat what never speaks.

Stand still.
And move only to stand.
And think only to gaze.
And wish only to rest.
And speak only to cease.

Statue of The Dying Gaul

Hushed be the dungeon stones, ever tongueless
Dwell the aerial alpine rocks, yet ne'er feel
We such anxious space as thy rigid peal
Ever sounds. Wicked mortal smite! Not less
A man, no, for humbly thy sagacious
Brow espies the secret but once revealed;
That mighty arm, which lately clenched brazen steel,
Trembles to uphold a swooning weakness;
Already far away, no one watches
Your heart's chaos pound forth thy broken side
Precious oil, nor witnesses forgotten
Moments rise in pander. With taut snatches
Quaking lungs bleed air, and then blur and wide
Hot the pirouetting world cries, and then –

 ## *Storm*

Churlish Nature withdrew her saucy gaze
And dropped her rainbow smile to a frown,
Shook her dark tresses oe'r those azure ways
And flashed resentful tears upon the ground;
Her swelling ire startles the swirling black
With quickened glances of revengeful light;
Her wicked screams whirl hawthorn forth and back,
And rend the shuddering heart of fearful night;
Anon she flays the teeming air of innocence,
Remorseless she, unbounded in restraint,
So flings a biting curse of earthly issuance
Full sudden at the dawn – then 'gins to faint...
      Her maddened locks hang limpid round her
          fires,
      As with feeble growls her moistened breath
          expires.

Dawn

Coy Aurora peeps her rosy eyelid
O'er the glowing rill, ungirds her sable silk,
And nimbly lights upon the cooling spread
Of emerald velvet. With fresh dewy milk
She laves her drowsy limbs, her perfumed curls
Waft teasing scents along the somber aisle
Of sylvan temple, cloying the bee-girls'
Nectar love, and rousing to choric guile
Twitter, shriek, warble, soft-cooing murmur,
The million wing-notes from Apollo's lyre.
And lo! Phoebus comes, regaling fervor,
As supine she awaits that sweeter fire.
      Her blazing Lord opes wide celestial heat,
      And fertile charms fill gushing Earth replete.

 ## *To Sleep*

A Reply to John Keats

No, Sleep, stay thy treacherous peace, suffuse
This heavy liquor through the twilight must
Of Earth's ferment, or bid thy drowsy Muse
Bedeck the horrid moon with opiate dust.
Why dab my lids with this gum illusion,
Just when the wind of day begins to fling
Aloft the lighter jewels of Reason?
For well I know thy wooing tongue may sing
A cunning, honey lay, engender trust
In tepid charms, and leave a clear vision
Of Memory's pearl rent by Siren lies.
Still – if thou must enshroud in mellow death
This weary corpse, let slip my airy eyes
To gaze in silence on my quiet breath.

It takes so long to fold an awkward sheet,
It takes so long to iron out a shirt,
It takes so long to bathe, and dress, and eat,
So long to settle upsets without hurt;
It takes so long to read a weary page,
It takes so long to read it yet again,
So long to meld our actions with our age,
So long to answer words with wordless ken;
It takes so long to understand an act,
It takes so long to see we never did,
Too long to feel the wrongs we can't retract,
Too long to know that nothing's ever hid.
         What is a life? We never had to wait:
         Just now, inhale this light our days create.

FIRST MOMENTS

At last I know I cannot find your death.
Your image framed, in fond remembrance hung,
Holds traces of a muted, sacred breath,
An ether song, in silent measures sung,
A hymn of Self, the Self we need not mourn.
So why ask, "Where are you" or "Whither hence"?
A lift between your cradled eyes newborn
Augurs clear the Child of our finer sense:
An infant love who glides about your gaze,
Who passes from your nostrils through your lips,
Declaiming to us in unspeaking praise
The secret love that from your body slips.
      Your love in death is what your lives release,
      May we let die what lets our love increase.

for Patricia, Stephan, Michael and Robert

My reasons run behind my Love's intent,
Pursuing "wherefore" with a promised "why";
But why pursue the reasons Reason spent
When she I love undoes them with a sigh?
A nuance melts the second 'tis expressed,
My pleas for succor forfeit what they seek,
These tailored gabbles, only when undressed,
Come near the artless blush upon her cheek.
And for I know a mouth is not a tongue,
And rounded measures measure only air,
Let fall the pen, and leave the song unsung,
But press those lips whose softness speaks all prayer.
    Yes, rather than encode my heart's surmise,
    I find my reasons in her loving eyes.

Love demands I know not who you are.
I never see you make your dreams dissolve,
Nor feel the hurt that shocks your heart ajar,
Which you with grace to gracious love resolve;
I cannot sit behind your tender eyes,
Admiring art and life as one tableau,
Nor rest in frank regard of wordless lies
Another's manners inadvertent show;
'Tis less to say a body is not soul,
Then know we share a touch, whose golden sheen
Divinely rounds us as a living whole,
An aura felt, and loved, though never seen.
       And now my aura begs to whisper this –
       Be silent now, this whisper is a kiss.

Someone said, your beauty misbehaves,
We lie seduced by promises unkept;
Someone said, your wisdom but enslaves,
Each thought unnurtured while our fancy slept;
And someone said you are not even there,
These gleams of glory or sublime sagesse
Just painted ciphers wrought from wishful air,
An empty surfeit, taking less from less.
All this is true – I never doubted so,
Nor looked for riches with a purpose blind,
But lived with wealth where it was wont to grow,
Between each protest that was left behind.
     So moves all joy, where doubters never stray:
     Men follow what they love, not what they say.

Mona Lisa

Pleasures she knew, and bears her sated joys
With the modest wisdom of a votaress;
Sorrows untold, swathed in a godlike poise
Subsuming tears, and scars, and soft caress –
Or, not this. A simple life, simply wise,
Eschewing flam and tumult for this peace
So gently dwelling in those wordless eyes,
Receiving what she pierces without cease.
Why must we always fail to know your art?
And fail to fathom your gaze eterne?
I come but to play a pauper's part:
We are not here to revel, but to learn
      That what you in pious silence teach,
        Surpasses all nor tongues nor pulpits preach.

[155]

Bemuséd Eros, lolling off to sleep,
Let droop about him his fiery darts;
A Vestal priestess chaste, of Dian's keep,
Stole off with one; her virgin sisters' hearts,
Startled by the arrow's immortal ray,
Their vigilance pure flooded with unknown flame,
Begged succor of their mistress to allay
The near-mad tremors furling joy with shame.
Demurring, she espied a fountain near
That fed a marble tub from spouts of gold,
And more to temper Love than votaries' fear,
She plunged the gleaming brand in waters cold –
     Those waters burbled hot: now to the pool
     Each naked came and bathed, Love's willing fool.

 ## *To Shakespeare*

Some men their rhymes a fictive name assign,
Creation of Creator winning fame;
Others let silence trail the final line,
Like Egypt's scribes, mute wonder their acclaim.
You perfectly did both, and more than this,
You let the world pick o'er your sacred verse,
To shift, expunge, rephrase, rewrite, dismiss,
Dubious charm of admiration's curse.
While scholars rifle shelves in search of you,
Your bequest eternal ever schools our life,
We live each day as you have taught us to,
Immortal striving built on mortal strife.
　　　　In truth, you never wrote a word. Your Art
　　　　Is in your Love, inscribed on every heart.

Macdougal Street

for Susan and Sally

What is a habit? That day it led me
Past all habit. Compelled by preference
I stepped out into the bright winter air
From the spiral stairwell descent, of which,
Curiously, an imprint lingers still,
Despite the dullness that frequency breeds,
And threaded my accustomed pathway
Along the avenue, through the terminal
Where movement from a bus drew up my gaze,
And there were Jim and Cookie, smiling, waving,
For them a hello (for me a farewell,
As I only later comprehended),
My heart at peace for their final union;
Then to a train, and to a bookshop,
My weekly ritual, my phantom tether –
More slenderly tenuous than I knew,
More magnificently solid than I knew –
Down the familiar aisle, scanning titles,
Reaching for the expected and finding
The Unexpected. Life stopped. And began.
I stepped out into the bright winter air,
Uplifted, giddy, buoyant, crossed the road,

A few feathered paces down the pavement
Passed into a pub, where the script began,
The curtain parted, every sight and sound
Messaging unknown magic; I hurtled,
Seated at that table, light-years away
And never looked back; home within my breast,
The slender needle-eye of chance traversed,
The immaculate, invisible point
Of unspeakably holy convergence:
A door – that place, that day, that hour, that habit.
Recalling now my youthful wanderings
Along that crowded street, rife with promise
But not a promise to me extended,
My heart searching it knew not why nor where,
Too alone to know what loneliness was,
Too naïve to life's ungrantable wishes;
Recalling now my visits to that spot,
Where work and play and movement carry on,
Where pub and bookshop tell no more their tale,
A tale told only by a grateful heart,
No longer seeking for the prize of words,
Living rather the hallowed prize untold.

Cassandra on the Aegean

Sharp the sudden rise and falling, every fall her body
    shaking,
Harsh the cold air wet and pelting, rainy mists conceal
    her tears;
Salt-sea gusts inciting shivers, searing thoughts her
    heart awaking,
A wounded heart inured to dread, shielded mute from
    fears by fears.

Beneath her blistered freezing feet, awkward planks
    heave with their creaking;
'Neath those planks the pond'rous thudding – waves,
    and oars, and rustling chains –
Keep pace a dire syncopation, with her sisters' moans
    unceasing,
A dirge to death and banishment, hopelessly discordant
    strains.

About her soldiers sway and slip, straining tight the
    anxious brailing,
As the wide sails bend and flutter, billowed taut with
    Diane's breath;
What the Goddess had denied them, when their
    nascent task was failing,

Now She grants as She denied them – glory won by
    virgin death.

Off either side, in sleek pursuit, each ship cleaves the
    foaming breakers,
Rushing sightless to their future, where they trust their
    solace lies,
Pounding drum-beats to remind them of the countless
    flaming acres
Razed to dust in guiltless triumph, smoke-filled fires in
    blood-red skies.

She eyes their swords, now sheathed in hide, cleansed
    of flesh torn from her siblings,
Lashed to their thighs unassuming, undisclosing what
    they'd wield –
More a dead heart than hand and arm, willing to
    impale our striplings;
More a soul conquered by conquest, to force the
    bleeding to yield.

That night she knew, and yet she slept, e'en her
    tortured heart subsiding,
Weary of the crowds who mocked her. Circled round
    their wooden doom,
Tossing flowers, chanting idylls, shrewish maids her
    omens chiding,
Youths their roiling flambeaus brandished what would
    soon their world consume.

Too oft she bowed to glazéd eyes, common sense to her
  explaining,
Friends and parents begging reason, mobs resounding
  reasoned lies,
Accepting anything revealed, save her steady vows
  refraining,
Stripped by a god to naked truth, uttered visions her
  demise.

To know what is and what shall be prepares us not for
  beholding;
What we expect, when manifest, shocks an Unknown
  world to birth.
Thus doth Phoebus' curse confound her: witness to
  divine unfolding,
To see as He, and crushed withal…timeless sight of
  mortal dearth.

That distant morn she heard the conch, faintly first,
  then pompous blowing –
Bumptious Paris playing at Pan. Sandals patt'ring,
  tinkling bells,
Girlish shrieks and gruff-throated men, soon the flutes
  and tambors growing,
Choric voices sweetly naïve: Poor Troy, awash with her
  spells.

For naught the Prophetess arose, stepped down to the
  portal silent;

For naught the retinue she heard – shuffles, murmurs,
    laughter rise –
Then at the threshold, solemn pause. She, for sight of
    horrors distant,
Scorned it all, 'til doorways opened: Sudden Beauty
    flushed her eyes!

Shall we adore, or ravish her! Possess who our heart
    possesses!
Golden wisps dapple her blushes, azure glimpses softly
    know
All looks caress her breasts and lips. Shyly she adjusts
    her tresses,
Bangles gently jingling, perfumed smiles her charms to
    all bestow;

Then a note at first unnoted: her luscious whispers,
    sweet respiring,
Seemingly but idle music, shaped itself in words
    sublime;
Harp-like tones, in subtle rhetoric, each succumbing
    ear inspiring,
Limpid discourse all arresting, tyranny suffused with
    rhyme.

No, Friend, Beauty is not stupid, though gently she may
    stupefy.
That day, of feasts and innocence, willingly was Troy
    laid waste;

What poets sung and masons cut, vainly sought to
    rectify
The hidden sin in victors' spoils: slowly lose what's won
    in haste.

Now as the stern armada speeds, from each hull the
    clamors sounding –
Women and girls shriek their sorrows, shake their
    irons, pound the boards,
Rouse in pitches base to alto, one impassioned chord
    abounding,
As would conjure Triton's fury, tempest floods to
    drown the hordes.

Unmoved, the king above her sits, shrouded in his
    forward staring;
She can't but smile at this figure, wrapped in soaking
    garments drear,
Helpless in his pose triumphant, he naively homeward
    bearing,
Knowing not this path of glory, once achieved shall
    disappear.

Blind to wind and freezing water, seeing naught but
    what's before him,
She can't but pity this conceit, majesty before the flood,
His robes now lank with rain and foam, soon to greet
    what does abhor him,
Leader of men drenched in water, soon now to be
    drenched in blood.

"Am I his lover? Am I wife? Must I gentle tendresse
    offer?
"Yield my warmth of arms and kisses? Let him quiver
    my delight?"
One glance more at that elder frail, all joys dissolve that
    she would proffer,
Not for his age, nor horrid fate, rather grief for
    deathless sight.

A youthful virgin supplicant, her first sacred vigil
    holding,
Alone, the silent tapers lit, midnight in that hallowed
    shrine,
Fragrant smoke from incense braziers, holy rites her
    virtues molding,
There her modest childhood ended, ravished by influx
    divine.

Set within a concave recess, stained glass windows
    darkly framing,
Apollo's marble image stood, solemn brooding over
    naught,
A sculptor's hand but proximate, Art's attempt the
    nameless naming;
To this stone she hymnals chanted, helpless words
    'gainst whom she fought.

Suddenly the glass illumined – golds, blues, greens,
    reds sprightly dancing –
Unearthly sunlight blazed all figures, animating
    outlined forms;

Then floating o'er the statue swelled a diamond sphere
    entrancing,
Swelling now between her heartbeats, immanent
    celestial storms.

Borders melted twixt her psyche, and these dire fiery
    breezes,
Thought and candle, hand and sorrow, all alike were
    objects strewn;
She felt the granite 'gainst her back, now this supine
    maid He seizes,
Mouth agape she cries out nothing, burning in
    Celestial Noon.

All solace stripped, all fancies shorn, all her brightest
    thoughts awaken,
Beholding what but piety, steeped in terror,
    understands –
How can Mortal bear Eternal? How to give what has
    been taken?
Forced to see all that man should not, banished to
    internal lands.

Abruptly upright she relents. Dark returns with muted
    waftings,
Wax-ends sputter, glass walls blacken, Phoebus' form a
    foolish doll;
Her foot soles cooling on the tiles, only silence hears
    her gaspings,
Her glowing breast her way illumines down the
    echoless hall.

Mortals adore all mortal dreams, solace that a Future
    beckons,
More so gaze at footsteps wandered, musing o'er
    nostalgia sweet;
Yet Future comes to Present lost, revealed not in years
    but seconds,
And the Past, although revealing, only shows what men
    repeat.

We seldom learn the secret stop, with which Time's
    unfolding ceases,
Hurtling hours and vanished moments but rankle our
    deeper dread;
To mark each grain of streaming sand, marks but how
    our dread increases,
No prophetic cipher needed knowing that our seconds
    fled.

But she, a fire caught in amber, glowing prisoned in the
    Present,
Neither longs for what invites her, nor begs former joys
    appear;
Sings she ever from Eternals, speaking truth to king
    and peasant,
Humbly sees horizons endless show her signs in sorrow
    clear.

Such became the Sun-God's imprint: eyes with clarity
    immuring,
Heralding what lies before her, sans the solace of belief;

Paeans to the passing eons, this terror humbly
   enduring,
All mortals shunning simple truth, that truth alone her
   relief.

Yet graver troubles was she spared: heedless ears her
   signs believing,
Acolytes her visions chanting, divinations etched in
   verse,
All knowledge save her cries dismissed, truth itself
   become deceiving –
Wisdom of Apollo knew, to worship her the greater
   curse.

So speeds onward this flotilla, brutal floods and
   tempests shunning,
Shudd'ring waves and icy lashings brushed aside in
   pursuit
Of kingly glories substanceless; he who fuels their
   anxious running
Throned aloft in naïve splendor, soon to savor barren
   fruit.

Behind him unawares she stands, lantern of dire
   Phoebus shining,
Bearing His immortal vision, blazing under sweet
   duress,
Her foreseeing self-beholding, helpless to events
   aligning,
Soon her final oath fulfilling, burden of the Prophetess.

Gaze on, O Tender Oracle! Suffer with your people
    banished!
Suffer more your omens silent, treading pathways yet
    untrod;
Soon your final chants shall tremble, once the world
    you knew has vanished –
You the sacrificial vestal, death that manifests the God.

The Parley of Age and Youth

"O Age, please tell me!" Youth did cry,
"Please speak your wisdoms true!
"How shall I live before I die?
"What should my time pursue,
"To end serene as you?"

Again cried Youth, "I fear the end,
"I fear the world unseen;
"My thoughts but feeble missives send
"Up to the voiceless sheen
"Of Heaven's silent mien.

"Where's Life Divine, O Father Age?
"Your answer please unfold!
"I see no puzzled anguish rage
"Upon your visage old –
"Leave not your gift untold."

With forehead creased and eyelids sere
A smiling Age replied,
"O Youth, dispel this needless fear,
"Let not mere doubtings chide
"A future yet untried."

Continued Age, "O naïve One,
"Your precious pleas relent.

"Look not to Life when Life's near done,
"Nor sift through hours now spent
"For which we must repent.

"Regale me, rather," Age implored,
"With strength, and health, and fun,
"With dreams and darlings you adored,
"As your life's path's begun
"Before a rising sun."

"But no, dear Father," Youth demurred,
"My dreams assurance need,
"When I behold my ventures lured
"Away to barren seed,
"Or prank a thoughtless deed."

The Young One frowned, "I beg respect
"For humors turned to stone,
"For many friends Youth's wiles neglect,
"Their lives to me unknown…
"So rues a heart alone."

Despite himself, Age broke a grin,
And said, "See what is old;
"It is not found on greying chin,
"Nor hands and fingers cold,
"Nor longings never told.

"Thy age," quoth Age, "Exceedeth mine,
"A shallow without core;
"Despite your pleas for Life Divine
"Thy lips espouse the lore
"Of musings wan and hoar."

"So can age end, my Agèd friend?"
Asked Youth with caustic lilt,
"Cast off the robings we pretend
"Have hid unsettled guilt
"For unknown treasures spilt?"

"That question begs its twin, fair Youth,
"Beware triumph in haste,
"Think not my years dissolved in ruth
"For days and hours erased –
" 'Tis Youth informs time's waste."

"A romping heart must stop itself?
"Is this your sage reply?"
"Nay, stop not there, include myself,
"Let you and I both die,
"Together." "O, but why?"

An age did Age in silence rest,
 His manner unperturbed;
Then to the strains in Youth's protest
 His sympathy averred
And spoke his final word:

"That midway life we must traverse,
"Where dreams and hopes are tried,
"Oft leaves men with Time's timeless curse:
"All love that we denied
"Was where those dreams abide.

"When you arrive at this, my hour,
"But bear a naked heart;
"The Living seek a lifeless dower,

"Arrayed with baubles smart
"To claim a life apart.

"Don't look for answers in my years,
"Nor doubt your own bright eyes,
"I only grant that mortal fears
"Of yearning for Life's prize
"Relent when yearning dies;

"So come." "I come, with final breath
"Returning yours and mine."
Then in the arms of Patient Death
Both Age and Youth enshrine
The Seal of Life Divine.

Prayer of the Golden Fox

One day while walking idle by a stream,
I heard a rustle from a nearby tree
Where, on its low-slung bough, a cock was perched;
He puffed and shook his coat of russet down,
Then arched his beak and crown up at the sky,
As though he would the muted heavens sound.
But my footfall snapped a twig, he jerked about,
And squawking pleaded, "Kind sir, your mercy,
"Please destroy me not! I have a burden
"My heart must now release. Finding no friend
"Nor peer about these woods, I sought alone
"To tell the winds and grasses, and these leaves,
"My meeting curious this early morn."
 Smiling at his false distress, I countered,
"Your life, my skittish one, is dear as mine,
"Your ardor, more pronounced. If you deem it well,
"Gladly would I join this nature theatre,
"And midst this verdure, hear your urgent tale."
To further quell his caution, at a glance
I spied a dry and hardened stump of oak,
And quick besat me like the final guest
Arriving a trice before curtain up.
Relieved, he filled his breast with dew-wet air,

53

Sighed and shook his plumèd layers, then billowed
Out like a feathered Buddha, and in tones
By turns prophetic and confused, began:
"At dayspring fresh met I a wanderer,
"A fox of noble mien, with poise refined,
"Sinews firm and full, his flaring nostrils
"Keen as was his gaze, his black ears a wasp
"A league away could he clearly detect,
"And no doubt ignore. Such bearing rarely
"Graced these woodlands, leonine majesty
"Alert and proud, yet with comportment staid;
"Even so, these qualities were surpassed
"By the brilliant enigma of his hide,
"A coat of gold, pure as robes imperial,
"Plush as regal carpets of woven silk
"Unfurled for dainty princess feet to tread.
"Even so –" here the cock suppressed a sob –
"Even so was this surpassed by his gaze,
"Which, when a glance became a look, a stare,
"I soon was lost, for deep within those eyes
"There sat an ancient, fathomless sorrow,
"An unsettled need devouring his heart
"That gripped his soul with roots of agéd pain,
"And forced my soul a terror to choke down – "
And now the rooster shuddered, mouth agape,
Tossed back his twitching, crested majesty,
As though to bellow clarions of grief.
But then his supple frame arrowed itself,
He stared at me an instant with renewed calm,

And whispered:
"Sudden then he spoke, and bade me mark
"His prayerful measures. My tale, sir, ends, and begins."
At this the cock surrendered up his charge,
And, unceremonious as air itself,
Recited the prayer of the golden fox:

O you of nervous feathers, fear me not. Despite your
stentorian reveille, I know you surpass many
creatures in the craft of listening and recall. Please
then to hear me articulate to you that which I
repeat to myself day and night, and day in night.
An attentive ear is among the dearest kindnesses we
of the living can bestow.
I do not want to speak.
I hear the chatter of crows,
The squawk of hens,
The hum of gnats,
The buzz of wasps,
The grunt of pigs,
The snorts of bull and horse and bison,
The growls of cougar and lion and dog,
And the unendurable, never-ending murmurs and
shouts and cackles and cries of the human creature.
All of these sounds are the merest of the mere: words. I
do not want words.

Words are my plague, my poison, my allure, my
death in life. Words explain the inane, describe

*the useless, emphasize the obvious, proselytize the
meaningless, dwell upon the uninteresting, and
obscure the essential.*

Words kill – the essential.

*Words, whose promises and plans die aborning,
whose yearnings end in besotted love of yearning
itself, whose endless questions inure us to simplest
answers and truths.*

*We speak words, and we starve. We speak words, and
we weep. We speak words, and we die.*

I want to sing. I want to become song.

I want to feel arise within me a sweet impulse of joy.

*I want this joy to push from my heart to my breath,
from my breath to my throat, from my throat to my
lips, and from my lips out into the all-embracing
air.*

*I want to hear my joy dance melodic, by turns sweet,
insouciant, sorrowed, inflamed, confused, assured.*

*I want a constant flush of feeling to become, as it
leaves my mouth, a full resplendent palette of
sound that shall please and enthrall all who hear,
and shall move me to abandon myself to this song,
this song not of me, but passing through me.*

I want to see. I want to become sight.

*I want what is before me to live as it is, as I see it now.
And I want what I see to be shared with others, that
they may see what I see, if only for a few moments.*

*I want not – O dear God – to describe, or explain...
but no more of that.*

We look at a painting for a few moments, and then look away. Or walk away. And then we come back and look again, and it is there, again, as we had left it; it is there, to be seen, again, just as it had been before, as he or she who painted it had seen it, and lived it, and imprinted it, before.

This I want, to represent a moment, a moment of what we see, and to have others see it, not for me but for themselves. And I want them to be able to return again and again, and always see it as for the first time.

I want to flow. I want to become water.

I want to become a creek. I want to trickle silently over glossy stones and into grassy plains, fill quiet rills and gentle pools, moisten the morning air, cool the bankside arbors, invite both fowl and beast to drink and plash and bathe.

I want to become a brook. I want to burble meaningless chuckles to passers-by, gurgle amusing nothings to men and ladies lying in lazed abandon on the grass, and spray a softened mist on all who lean their faces close to mine.

I want to become a stream. I want to gather myself and rush with increasing confidence toward an unknown glen, or rocky runnel, or even over an unseen edge. And as I grow stronger, I want my stream to become a river.

I want this river to journey into mystery, and be at once the journey and the mystery. And I want

*others to follow where I lead them, assured that
resting upon and gliding along my flowing wisdom,
a wisdom that comes of having led, having been led,
and able to lead anew, shall take them where they
need to go.*

*And I want to become the ocean, I want to become the
emptying into the ocean, that point of arrival that
is never arrival, that is always foment and mystery
and the restless efflux and afflux where eternity
and infinity forever conjoin.*

I want to fly. I want to become wind.

*I want to scud in breezes like a mischievous imp,
gliding in easy frolic over plains, betwixt mountain
passes, across mighty seas, and through mysterious
jungles.*

*I want to tease about the ears of timid statesman,
uninspired poet, sleepless peasant, unfound belovéd,
scorned exile, pensive thinker, solitary lover, and
whisper to each the private secret that will unlock
what now so enchains their despair.*

*I want to steal my way in and through the nose
and mouth of every fearful heart and reluctant
mind, and help them push forth from the hesitant
threshold of speech, the one singular utterance they
each must impart to the one or the sundry who
must receive it.*

*I want to whistle about the crowds in street or temple,
and bear for them the symbol of all that with
certainty is, but can never be touched or seen. And*

to help each one in that crowd to believe and to
trust what never can be touched or seen.
And then at last I want to rise into the stratospheric
  land of no law save the one my next capricious
  movement creates. And so reside in tranquil
  agitation with my whirling companions, where we
  forever merge and love, and forever learn from the
  starlight divine ever pouring its infinite wisdom
  from galactic eternity upon our humble dome of air.

I want to burn. I want to become light.
I want to burn quietly in the pendent air. I want to
  rest a glowing circle in azure day and sable night,
  an eternal silent disk, whose ever-present eye
  assures each woman and man that what they seek
  outside themselves awaits them at some certain
  moment of "shall be."
And wherever I reside in the infinite land of space and
  time, I want my circle of light to become a realized
  sphere. A sphere of fire that burgeons at once in all
  directions, that in divine simultaneity destroys and
  fashions anew an infinite array of living forms and
  worships. A self-reflecting sphere who witnesses the
  enigma of all that lives and dies, and the grander
  enigma of what never will.

As troubled as the cock had been
At outset of his tale reluctant,
So now with manner mild and pacific
He tilted down at me a friendly look,

59

And said:
"A miracle, sir, it was to witness
"His tortured throes melt to haloed verses.
"Throughout his speech I lingered on his eyes,
"And watched them slowly yield their darker edge,
"Watched each impulse of his prayer gleam and flicker
"About his gradually widening sight,
"Gradating in joyous certainty –
"Nudge by phantom nudge – out from hardened ire
"Into those ether pastures he longed for.
"And after his hushed 'What never will,'
"This noble fox, regal with humility,
"Glanced up at me a tender, silent farewell,
"Turned and padded softly through the brush,
"His lustrous raiment gliding like water
"Betwixt shades and shoots and waving grass,
"And vanished in Forever's certainty."
No more than a gapless breath elapsed
After these final words. The rooster then
Abruptly stretched himself, lithe and supple,
Leapt and hopped up several swaying branches
To the topmost limb; once there, he flapped out
His wings a span to rival the boldest eagle,
Grew asudden several times his girth,
And launched himself into the forest air;
He glided leisurely in quiet stillness,
A shrinking silhouette against the clouds,
Then flapped a final thrust away unseen.
And ever since, I wander in these woods
Alert, no longer idle, always keen

To drink in with joy the neighborhood trills
Of sparrow, lark, redbreast, swallow, and finch;
To behold sans indifference or greed
This hour's tableau of color, light and form;
To dip my hands in cold running waters,
Bidding these gentle wavelets sweet adieu,
As ripples fresh repleasure the instant;
To heed the teeming branches' orisons,
Secret pregnant whispers about my ears,
Majestic roarings in the upper skies;
And to forever behold each morning –
With meek but delicious anticipation –
Unfurl like woven silk the golden dawn.

A Little Red Flower

A little red flower, bobbing
In the gentle breeze, sunlight
Dappling the rustling blades and burrs
About her. I stooped down and asked,
"How do you, little red flower,
"Survive this rough and callous world?
"So naively bright and playful,
"You cavort insouciant in winds
"That push and flap your petals fair
"Where and how and as they please,
"Your simple charm no warder off
"Of weeds and vines and beetle fang;
"And soon a lass in merry haste
"Plucks you up, sports you in her locks,
"Leaves you to dry upon a sill,
"Then sets you in a secret page
"Where you for years, an age, will sleep
"Until, in absence, her tresses
"Grey, her eyesight dim, she, leafing
"Idly through her glee and sorrow,
"Finds you, fingers your papered crown,
"And sighs and seals you back again."

A little red flower, lilting
 Softly in the wavering light,
 Tipped aloft her scarlet bounty,
 Eyed me curious and asked,
"How do you, sir, of brow and arm,
"Survive this rough and callous world?
"So bravely flames your morn's intent,
"Escorted by a firm undoubt,
"Your goals and duty flood your days
"And trample o'er both wish and whimsy,
"And neither dreams, nor hopes, nor wit
"Replace a sad or vacant heart;
"And soon in haste your hurried life
"Plucks away the joy you reached for,
"Leaving your days but random sheets
"Half-read, half-written, barely known,
"Until that dreaded second comes
"Where you will go where you breathe not,
"Suddenly shunted past all sense,
"No single light to guide you there.
"And all this while, I smile at you,
"And bid you stay and dance with me."

Acknowledgements

Thank you to Ruth Atkins, Susan Luccini, John Craig, Charles Rodkoff, and my wife Solee for reading these poems and offering their honest comments, both general and finely detailed, all of which I am very grateful for.

Thank you to Solee for the drawing gracing the cover of this book, and to William Bentley for another wonderful book design.

A special thank you to Jonathan Beth, for generously lending me the inspiring writings of his late brother, Ilan.

If I lay me down to sleep
The devil lures me to the deep,
But when his lies
Renew my rise
I bless the Light that grants me eyes.

MR. WILLIAM SHAKESPEARES

176 MacDougal Street New York, New York

LUNCHEON FARE

Soups
- Onion Soup Gratinee — 2.25
- Soup of the day — 1.75
- Chili — 2.25

Salads
- Spinach - with a warm bacon dressing — 3.95
- Shakespeares House Salad with shrimp, scallops and flaked crabmeat with an anchovy dressing — 5.95
- Salad Bar - as an Entree — 3.95

Potato Bumpkins
A huge fluffy baked potato filled with your choice of the following
- Shepherds Stew
- Turkey Suprema
- Chili with Cheddar — 3.95
★ Served with unlimited Salad bar.

Pub Sandwiches
- Barbecued Beef — 3.95
- Steak Sandwich — 7.95
- Club Sandwich — 4.95
- French Dip au Jus — 4.95
- Turkey — 4.50
- Bacon, Lettuce and Tomato — 3.50
- Grilled Cheese plain — 3.25
      with bacon and tomato — 3.95
★ Above served with unlimited salad bar.

English Dinner
- Shepherds Pie — 4.95
- Fish and Chips - in ale batter — 4.95
★ above served with unlimited salad bar.

The Sideboard
- Deep Fried Zucchini — 1.75
- Onion Rings — 1.50
- Steak Fries — 1.50
- Chili — 2.25

Quiche
- Lorraine — 3.95
- Broccoli — 3.95
- Chefs Choice — 3.95

Omelettes
- Mushrooms and Swiss — 4.25
- Cheddar Cheese — 3.95
- Chefs Choice — 4.50
   above served with peach half and choice of bagel or Muffin

Bardburgers
THE Publick house specialty
- The Hamlet - with sauteed onions and peppers, cheddar cheese and bacon — 3.95
- The Guildenstern - with sauteed mushrooms and mozzarella cheese — 3.95
- THE Rosencrantz - with melted cheddar, canadian bacon and tomato — 3.95
- The Othello - with cheddar or swiss cheese — 3.95
- The London Pair - hamburger and flaked crabmeat each on a english muffin — 5.95
- The Bardburger - plain with lettuce and tomato — 3.75
★ all above served with unlimited salad bar.

Hearty Barbecue
- Barbecued Chicken Breast- broiled and lightly basted with our special sauce — 6.95
- Barbecued Baby Back Ribs - a tender rack of ribs broiled and basted with our special sauce — 7.95
- Ribs and Chicken Combination Try them both — 7.95
★ all above served with unlimited salad bar.

A Good Ending
- Carrot Cake, Cheese Cake, Pecan Pie or Chefs Choice of the day — 2.25
- Apple Spice Cake or English Cake Pudding — 1.95